3.70 art

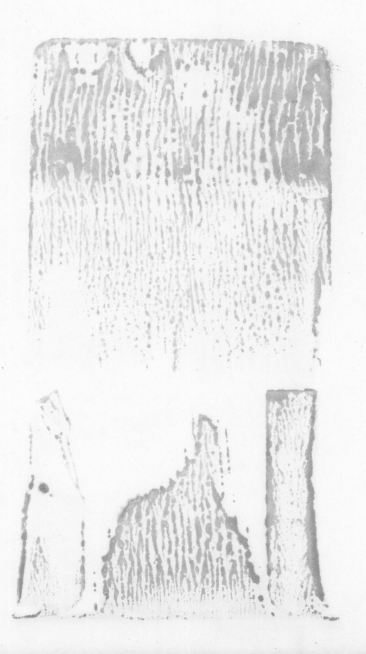

ROOFS OVER AMERICA

ROOFS

Lothrop, Lee & Shepard Co., Inc., New York

OVER AMERICA
by Marion Downer

Copyright © 1967
by Lothrop, Lee & Shepard Co., Inc.
Library of Congress Catalog Card Number: 67-15711
Printed in the United States of America

To my sister Tat

ROOFS OVER AMERICA

Roofs and People

The word roof has been briefly defined: "protection for an interior." And this is accurate whether the roof is the snow and ice on the top of an igloo or the layers of soil over an underground burrow.

Such roofs seem to be completely satisfactory in places where time stands still. But in America, a very adaptable race of people have been building roofs of various kinds for almost four centuries, and making themselves at home beneath each kind.

Roofs tell their story of the times and the people.

PART I

AMERICA'S FIRST ROOFS

Seventeenth Century

The Saddle Roof at Cape Cod

There were no sheltering roofs for new arrivals when the May-flower landed in 1620. But as soon as the colonists could chop down trees and stand logs on end for walls, they roofed them with branches in the arched saddle shape.

The thatch of twigs and reeds on these roofs often blew away in hurricane winds. Sometimes blazing Indian arrows set them on fire. At last, with much hard work, boards were made, shingles were split, and in a few years the New England Cape Cod cottage had evolved. The roofs were especially high-pitched to shed heavy snow in long winters.

One of the first of these roofs was on the Aptuxcet Trading Post, which had been located where traders could bring furs by land or water and store them for shipment to Europe, thus contributing to the prosperity of the Plymouth Colony. Governor Bradford mentioned the building in his history—"They built a house theire and kept some servants who also raised some corne and reared some swine."

A Cape Cod Cottage. The Aptuxcet Trading Post, Bourne, Massachusetts, built in 1627.

Photograph by Hugo G. Poisson

The Salt-Box House

Building houses was hard work, accomplished under many difficulties. Trees had to be felled and split, all with a few crude tools.

As more colonists arrived and families grew bigger, more house room was needed. The roofs must provide more shelter.

Extending one sloping half of a roof outward was a way of making more space with only a little more work. When that was done, a house had the unbalanced shape that made it resemble the wooden salt box used in the kitchens of that day. But under the extended part of the roof there was space for an extra room.

One substantial salt-box house was built on a beautiful windswept island. It had all the improvements of the time and was a wedding gift from the groom's father who gave the land and from the bride's father who built the house.

A shingled Salt-Box House, Nantucket Island, Massachusetts, built by Jethro Coffin in 1650.

Photograph by Bill Haddon

The Stone-End House

Coastal winds were sometimes strong enough to blow down the settlers' wooden houses. The widened base of the salt-box house gave it some solidity but not enough. No better shape could be contrived, and there was no material to use except what was right there along the shore.

Then a way was found to secure the walls to the ground and the roof to the walls. It called for ingenuity and hard work.

Strong horizontal roof beams were wedged into an end wall built of stones cemented together with plaster made of ground-up sea shells. This framework was impossible to jar and the long part of the salt-box roof was anchored to it.

The chimney built into the stone end was extra large. The fireplace inside was broad and deep enough to hold large logs.

A Stone-End House known as the Clemence House, Manton, Rhode Island, built in 1654.

Photograph from the collections of the Library of Congress

15

The Long Roof

The chimney with its fireplace was usually built at the end of a house. But much of its heat was lost on the out-of-doors side of it. When the chimney was built through the center of a long roof, the fireplace at its base sent heat two ways inside the house.

The long roof of John Alden's house shows an example of a centered chimney. Windows built close beneath the roof's edge gave ventilation.

John Alden had been a cooper in England. His skillful repair work on the Mayflower kept it afloat on the trip. He became a magistrate of the Plymouth Colony and was too busy to build a good house for himself. Finally, in 1653, his fifth son, Jonathan, built this one strongly and well.

The John Alden House, Duxbury, Massachusetts, built by Jonathan Alden, fifth son of John and Priscilla, in 1653.

Photograph by courtesy of Charles W. Alden

The Gambrel Roof

A long, high-pitched roof had an almost unusable part inside its peak where a head would be bumped if anyone tried to stand upright. A way to provide more headroom was invented by a change in roof design.

A lengthwise rise in each sloping side made the outer parts of a roof pitch steeply and the other parts near the ridge pole flatten out slightly. That angled bulge gave what is called the gambrel roof. It allowed height inside for upstairs bedrooms in much the way a mother hen adjusts her wings to cover her sleepy brood.

At the Fairbanks House, oldest home now remaining in New England, each son who married brought his bride to live in a new wing that had been built especially for him. These wings had roomy gambrel roofs.

One Wing of the Fairbanks House, Dedham, Massachusetts, built in 1636.

Photograph by courtesy of the Fairbanks family.

The Overhang Construction

Many of the colonists were experienced builders. One type of house they made dates back to England's middle ages. The style of construction is called the overhang. An arched roof and two top floors were set onto a very strong floor that extended slightly beyond the lower part of the house, forming a narrow secondary roof over the door.

These three-floor houses were built at intervals along borders of settlements where troops were garrisoned for defense against Indian raids. Each of these garrison houses was kept occupied by a family who was willing and capable of taking in all the defenseless neighbors in times of danger, and feeding and bedding them down until the crisis was over.

A Garrison House overhang type of construction, Early Colonial.
Photograph from the collections of the Library of Congress

Gabled Roofs

Along the coast of Cape Cod, shipowners made good use of the overhang style of house by adding gables. A large, rambling house might have several wings with a gable at the end of each.

Gables were not exactly an origination. The people in the colonies at this time did not care to have new ideas in any of their possessions.

A house with gables was reminiscent of Old England, and they made a sea captain less lonely in a new land with the wide ocean on one side and miles of unknown country on the other He could climb to whichever gable gave him the best view to watch for ships on the far horizon or to count his own at anchor in the harbor.

The House of Seven Gables, Salem, Massachusetts, built by John Turner, mariner, in 1668.

Photograph/Ewing Galloway

The Dormered Roof

Plantation owners in Virginia and Maryland were as prosperous as the shipowners of northern ports. But they lived, during the first years of colonization, in modest cottages patterned after those in English villages. The shingled roofs had English-style brick chimneys and tiny dormer windows, each with its own peaked roof to cap it.

The cottages were beautiful and in all ways adequate for life where serenity and sociability prevailed. Much visiting went on between the widely separated plantation homes. Families traveled either in carriages, on horseback, or in boats along the shores of estuaries. They carried many bags and baskets, and songs and poetry recitations enlivened their trips.

Approached from a distance, only the roof of this low house would be seen among surrounding trees. But its proportions gave promise of hospitality.

The Adam Thoroughgood House, Princess Ann County, Virginia,
built in 1636.

Photograph from the collections of the Library of Congress

The Dutch Roof

At about the time when the planters were building English cottage roofs in Virginia, Dutch roofs were rising in the New Amsterdam Colony. The first Dutch colonists had arrived, in what is now New York Harbor, in 1624. Even the first boat-load was well equipped with workmen and tools. Soon rows of little houses appeared with sharp gable ends pointing toward quickly constructed streets.

When another ship arrived with thirty families in it, groups were assigned by the colony to farm lands, and one went up the Hudson River. There, forts were needed because the Mohican Indians were apt to disregard peace agreements. The house shown here was a home that could serve as a fort for storing arms, and there were loopholes in the walls ready for pointing guns that could open fire if necessary.

The style of any house built by the Dutch was copied exactly from those in the homeland. Tile roofs, pointed gables without projecting eaves, and walls of excellent brickwork were the unfailing rule. There was no other embellishment.

Fort Crailo, Rensselaer, New York, built in 1642.

Photograph from the collections of the New York Historical Society

27

PART II

ROOFS
WITH A TOUCH
OF
ELEGANCE

Eighteenth Century

Roof With a Deck

In the 18th century, the sons of many families were sent to Europe after their graduation from college. The sojourns were for pleasure, but also to round out their education and add avenues of culture. They offered an opportunity for young men, future American citizens, to meet distinguished people and to acquaint themselves with European literature, music, art and social customs.

Above all, the young men were instructed to observe architecture, and one result of this cultural broadening was that soon afterward houses were built in America which were copies of those fashionable in London. The architectural style was elegant in the perfection of its balanced details and was called Georgian, meaning the time of King George III.

Some of the seaboard houses had a maritime touch at the top portion of the roof, made flat like a deck and enclosed with a white railing. On this "widow's walk" a sea captain's wife could pace and watch far out over the harbor where signal flags were raised whenever a homecoming fleet was sighted. It was assumed that at least one ship in a fleet would be lost in the crossing.

Longfellow House, Cambridge, Massachusetts, built in 1759.

Photograph by Preindl/Monkemeyer

The Symmetrical Style

On the strong, logically proportioned roof of this house the measured placing is almost painfully exact. Chimneys, dormer windows, a centered pediment and little decorative urns are all in balance. The balance continues on the house front with windows placed two by two and white columns edging the door.

From roof to doorstep, the English customs of building were dutifully followed. But if this house could have been placed beside some London house of the time, a certain American ruggedness would have distinguished it. Its walls of native stone would have looked rough beside the smooth British brick.

This difference and the similarities are the more interesting when it is remembered that on this ground George Washington's soldiers gave almost unbelievably tough resistance against the English, for whom they had exceedingly high regard in most matters.

The Benjamin Chew House, Germantown, Pennsylvania, built in 1763.

Photograph/Pennsylvania State Department of Commerce

33

A Greek Revival House

The roof of this 19th century house did not have the spreading slant that most earlier roofs had had. It was flat and hidden by a balustrade that edged its square sides, continuing over a deepset portico. The style of the house was Greek Revival, the style that was an important influence on all Southern mansions of that time. Greek design was creating enthusiasm everywhere abroad because of the Elgin Marbles that had been brought from Greece to the British Museum in London.

Although the balustrade around the roof was not Greek in design, its right angles and its height helped to carry out Greek temple proportions and gave stateliness. Tall white columns with Ionic capitals were authentically Greek.

This house with its classical dignity has been an appropriate place for the painting exhibitions which have been held here several times in the well-proportioned galleries beneath its broad roof.

The Roper House, Charleston, South Carolina, built in 1838.

Photograph from the collection of the Carolina Art Association, Gibbes Art Gallery

The Mansard Roof

There was a type of house flourishing briefly in America that was distinguished definitely by its roof. It was called the house with the Mansard roof.

The style had come from Paris where it had been invented for the purpose of avoiding a city tax levied on houses according to the number of floors they had. The Mansard roof, slanting backward from the walls of a house, was counted only as a half floor or attic, although it had windows in its sides.

However, a tax was not the reason for its popularity in America. Fashion had somehow approved the Mansard roof. It had a desirable city air.

Cities were spreading their borders. Their edges were a blending of town and country. At these edges, large houses built with Mansard roofs were sometimes left on unfrequented roads, out of step with progress. Fiction writers have often chosen them as settings, especially for their mystery stories.

America was changing. All roofs of yesterday would soon take their places in the historic past.

House with a Mansard Roof, Rhode Island, built about 1850.

PART III

CITY
ROOFS

Passing Roofs

When the 19th century was waning, houses could be found jumbled together at a city's edge, looking as if they had been washed there by a flood. Each roof could be seen to have lines derived from the earliest houses in America—the Cape Cod roof, the gambrel, the gabled roof, and even the dormered cottage.

Sometimes inappropriate additions resulted in misshapen roofs, but no new style had yet supplanted the old.

Fringe Area of a Metropolis, New York City, 19th century.

Photograph by Botwick/Monkemeyer

Narrow Roofs

Even in the days when carriages trundled on city streets, ground space in the heart of town was so limited that houses were squeezed together like dominos in a box. Each house was narrowed to make room for more houses with flat, narrow roofs.

These houses were family residences, and in spite of the crowding, they had a great deal of dignity and a kind of 19th century liveliness. Rear windows opened on gardens. Street windows had deep sills with folding inside shutters. Entrance halls had marble floors and hardwood stair rails along the squeezed stairs.

But as time went on, the narrow strips of ground beneath those narrow roofs were so highly taxed that families could not maintain the houses. At last, when they were nearly a century old, they were re-planned into apartments where many people could live. Tenants who had an artistic turn of mind regarded the houses as inimitable antiques.

Section of a city block, New York City, houses of the
early 19th century.

Photograph by Lida Moser/Monkemeyer

Skylight Roofs

Many of the narrow old houses lined the streets of New York's Greenwich Village. Their top floors, once used for the house-maids and children of families, were undesirable as apartments because there were so many stairs to climb. Ceilings were low, with light coming only from dormer windows.

This was at a time when young people of artistic talent were flocking to New York from every part of the country. Always lacking in funds, they needed inexpensive studios. So they took the flights of stairs in long leaps, had the landlords build skylights on the roofs, and there they painted under good north light.

A roof studio gave a feeling of being far removed from ordinary life. But these old roofs, here today, would be gone tomorrow.

Old House with Skylight Studio, Greenwich Village, New York City.

From the sketch book of Marion Downer

Forest of Roofs

An American metropolis, seen from above, shows a ragged mixture of rooftops both old and new, all standing together like a forest where no ground space is left bare underneath.

This crowding had been increasing for fifty years in highly populated cities when, in the early 1900's, boatloads of immigrants began arriving. Hundreds of thousands came each year.

Many of the men had left their native lands to avoid conscription in the armies. Many had hoped that the "land of the free" would have prosperity to share and places for their families to live. There was a welcome carved at the base of the Statue of Liberty—"Send these, the homeless, tempest-tost to me. I lift my lamp beside the golden door!"

New York was at that doorway.

But even a generous land could offer little work for inexperienced immigrants. Only the oldest and most run-down houses could offer shelter within the reach of almost empty pockets.

Unhealthy slums developed. New roofs, new homes, were desperately needed. But as to building space within the city, there was none. Then, in 1934, the first Municipal Housing Authority was created. It provided for slum clearance.

Skyview of new and old buildings, New York City, 20th century.

Photograph/Black Star

Tumbling Roofs–
Urban Renewal

Before new houses could be built, row upon row of old houses had to be cleared away. Demolition cranes began their wreckage on the old narrow roofs; then bulldozers rammed brownstone walls. Large areas of ground were reduced to rubble. Space was opened for urban renewal.

City planners and architects drew up plans for an entirely new kind of housing, based on projects in the Scandinavian countries and England. America's problem was greater—to put roofs over the heads of the most concentrated population in the world. At last, with the ingenious use of ground space, a high degree of success was attained.

The roofs of one successful housing project, seen from above, show a unique plan. Both neighborliness and privacy were considered. Windows never look into windows, and the ground is as open as possible for lawns and paths. No traffic enters this housing area. Children have a playground right at home. There is sun and air and pleasing color—elements found possible even in high-density living.

Stuyvesant Town, New York City, completed in 1948.

Photograph by Statile/Monkemeyer

Staggered Roofs

Other housing projects in the early sixties show the extreme economy of plan used in building low-rental apartments. A close-up view of roofs, and simultaneously of the ground below, is evidence of the good judgment used in a staggered arrangement.

Buildings with many floors are set, not flat against a street, but at a more interesting slant and at angles to each other. This allows as much diversity of appearance as possible in an extremely clean-cut layout.

Trees will never reach the rooftops as they did growing around houses of earlier days, but shrubs and lawns can alleviate the Spartan plainness prevalent in 20th century architecture.

Municipal Housing Units, New York City, early 1960's.

Photograph by Flying Camera Inc./Frederic Lewis

High-Rise Apartments

The population of the United States had long been recorded as two-thirds rural and one-third city dwellers. During the 20th century, urban population took the lead until the proportion is now completely reversed.

Added to the number of city-dwelling Americans, many people had come from foreign countries for professional work or for specialized study. To house them all, enormous apartment buildings were going up from coast to coast. They took the name, high-rise apartments.

Their flat roofs, out of sight from street level, have coverings of tar, gravel or asphalt, and sometimes of stainless steel.

The high-rise apartment building shown here is of a special type called by architects "slab construction." The boxlike shape has great height and width but is shallow in depth. Walks and lawns surround it, so that it stands apart from other architecture, looking free, although it holds almost six hundred apartments.

Facade of Apartment Building, Kips Bay Area, New York City, 20th century.

Photograph by Dan J. McCoy/Black Star

Repeated Units

Beauty is given slight importance where extreme practicality is the designer's only rule. On many city streets, high-rise apartment buildings stand in tiresome practical rows, all as similar one to another as sugar lumps placed on end.

To the passerby, they offer no enjoyment. Only sameness meets the eye.

Perhaps a warning has come just in time from scientists who say that visual monotony is psychologically harmful and deadening. The mind seeks variety and is frustrated by unrelieved repetition.

Row of Apartment Buildings, Chicago, Illinois, 20th century.

Photograph by Hays/Monkemeyer

Angled Roof Line

Monotony can be avoided in various ways. Sometimes it is managed by utilizing the ground space in an unusual way. Here the roof, designed by the architect, was angled so that the main walls of the building spread apart. Neither half is flat against the street.

Commercial building materials are tiresomely practical. There is no texture of natural wood and stone. There is no paint to give color. As planned here, shadows cast by light give variety of tone. The shadows repeat rhythmically and give a sort of texture to the building as a whole.

Apartment Building, Brooklyn, New York, 20th century.

Photograph by DiJordan Wilson/Pix

Curving Contours

Monotony is avoided when a building spreads its walls in curving lines like a huge bolt of ribbon unrolling. Its roof will whip around against the sky, and a sidewalk below it will have the same curves in its directions. For anyone walking there, this variation adds interest.

Apartment Building, Philadelphia, Pennsylvania, 20th century.

Photograph by Kerwin Roche/Monkemeyer

Round Roofs in the Sky

To reach light and air, what is better than a tower? To conserve land space, a tower cannot be excelled.

These possibilities were achieved in a building where sixty floors of apartments were placed on a small circular area of land and rose into a cylindrical tower with a round roof. Not only one was built, but two, and a term used for such compact living is megamopolitan.

Ground space, once assumed to be the birthright of every human being, is now a very limited commodity in cities. To utilize every inch of it and also create astonishing modern design is the achievement here.

Marina Towers, Chicago, Illinois, 20th century.

Photograph by Bernard Silberstein/Monkemeyer

PART IV

MODERN COUNTRY ROOFS

New Roofs for a Wide Land

Houses are designed by architects who know that buildings must have esthetic relationship with settings. The broad expanse of the American continent has every kind of landscape to offer. There are wave-washed beaches, wide prairies, rocky shores, wooded islands, rolling hills and flat fields.

Modern transportation has shortened distances. Building materials are never too far away. Many limitations of other ages have been removed along with many design conventions. This is a new day for new roofs over America.

Top Knot Tile Roof

Martha's Vineyard, Massachusetts

This is original, this is art—four square roofs over the four square parts of a T-shaped house. Each square roof is made of four triangles pitched upward and boxed off with small constructions dubbed "topknots."

65

PHOTOGRAPHER, JACK STERLING/ARCHITECT, W. BYRON IRELAND

Roof With Shingled Hoods

Ireland Residence, Columbus, Ohio

The two hood-shaped parts of this roof are wood shingled and are joined together by a small backward-slanting part over a glass wall. Unique.

The hood-covered rooms, one a studio and one a master bedroom, have side walls tilted in the way cozy attics sometimes are. Their sheltering fronts cover balconies from which there is a wooded landscape view.

66

PHOTOGRAPHER, EZRA STOLLER/ARCHITECTS, EDDMAN AND SALZMAN

*Paperfold
Roof*

New York State

This roof, shaped like a strip of paper that has been folded and then spread, is really a very strong type of construction. Each section of it is braced against the ones at its sides for dependable solidity. The extending points at top give a sunshade effect. Casual individuality.

67

Sloping Shed Roofs

New Jersey

Shed roofs slope out of sight on the four geometrical forms of this house. The backward slant differs for each part, also the height. Their tops are covered with white limestone chips.

The glassed-in fronts open on an ever-changing view of the ocean. Sculpturally dramatic.

68

Umbrella Roof

Colorado

This umbrella roof, though it is flat, not curved, gets its name from a center support that is like an umbrella stick.

Flat roofs are prime factors in much modern architecture because they can cover walls that stand at various angles. Here, walls of glass face the Rocky Mountains.

69

*Old Farm
Style Roofs*

Pennsylvania

A craftsman-like roof covers this home where separated parts are arranged in village or farmyard grouping. Though completely modern, the roof is made to appear as if it has been built onto at different times and the house has taken on a lived-in look. There is plate glass and, in contrast, rough stone walls.

70

Old Style Gable Roof

California

This sharply pointed and shingled roof reaches high on the craggy bank of an ocean's edge. The home has the effect of an old and casually built tree house. But terraces, almost level with the eaves, place it in the modern class.

71

PHOTOGRAPHER, R. WENKAM/ARCHITECTS, WIMBERLY,
WHISENAND, ALLISON & TONG, ARCHITECTS, LTD., OF HONOLULU, HAWAII

An A-Frame Roof

Honolulu, Hawaii

Good architecture is abstract art.

Centuries before the time of the Polynesians, Plato observed the principle: "Straight lines and circles and shapes made from them by lathe, ruler and square—these are beautiful always and absolutely."

This contemporary two-story house in Hawaii expresses this principle. It is the A-frame house. It was once constructed of poles lashed together and covered shaggily with grass.

Today, although the frame, roof, ceiling and most of the walls are made of steel and concrete, this ancient shape is not unlike the saddle roof on the Cape Cod house, one of the very first roofs in America.

72

Books Recommended For Further Reading

PART I

Lyman, Susan E., *The Story of New York*. New York, Crown Publishers, 1964.

Robinson, Ethel Fay and Thomas P., *Houses in America*. New York, The Viking Press, 1936.

PART II

Corbett, P. E., *The Sculpture of the Parthenon*. Baltimore, Penguin Books, 1959.

Eberlain, Harold D., and Cortlandt, VanDyke Hubbard, *American Georgian Architecture*. London, Pleides Books Limited, 1952.

Pevsner, Nikolaus, *The Englishness of English Art*. New York, Frederick A. Praeger, 1955.

PART III

Cantacuzino, Sherban, *Great Modern Architecture*. New York, E. P. Dutton & Co., 1966.

Rasmussen, Steen Eiler, *Experimenting Architecture*. Cambridge, The M.I.T. Press, 1964.

PART IV

Richards, J. M., *An Introduction to Modern Architecture*. Baltimore, Penguin Books (a Pelican Book), 1963.

Rudofsky, Bernard, *Architecture Without Architects*. New York, Museum of Modern Art, Doubleday & Co., 1965.

THIS BOOK WAS SET IN *Janson* & *Perpetua* TYPES BY *Sweetman Typesetting Corporation*, SOUTH HACKENSACK, NEW JERSEY. IT WAS LITHOGRAPHED BY *Halliday Lithograph Corporation*, WEST HANOVER, MASSACHUSETTS AND BOUND BY *American Book-Stratford Press*, NEW YORK. TYPOGRAPHY BY *Victoria Gomez*